Great Works **Instructional Guide for Literature**

Their Eyes Were Watching God

A guide for the novel by Zora Neale Hurston
Great Works Author: Jennifer Kroll

SHELL EDUCATION

Publishing Credits

Corinne Burton, M.A.Ed., *President*; Emily R. Smith, M.A.Ed., *Editorial Director*; Lee Aucoin, *Multimedia Designer*; Stephanie Bernard, *Assistant Editor*; Don Tran, *Production Artist*; Amber Goff, *Editorial Assistant*

Image Credits

Shutterstock (cover)

Standards

© 2007 Teachers of English to Speakers of Other Languages, Inc. (TESOL)
© 2007 Board of Regents of the University of Wisconsin System. World-Class Instructional Design and Assessment (WIDA)
© Copyright 2010. National Governors Association Center for Best Practices and Council of Chief State School Officers. All rights reserved.

Shell Education

5301 Oceanus Drive
Huntington Beach, CA 92649-1030
http://www.shelleducation.com
ISBN 978-1-4258-8997-5
© 2015 Shell Educational Publishing, Inc.

Table of Contents

How to Use This Literature Guide

Today's standards demand rigor and relevance in the reading of complex texts. The units in this series guide teachers in a rich and deep exploration of worthwhile works of literature for classroom study. The most rigorous instruction can also be interesting and engaging!

Many current strategies for effective literacy instruction have been incorporated into these instructional guides for literature. Throughout the units, text-dependent questions are used to determine comprehension of the book as well as student interpretation of the vocabulary words. The books chosen for the series are complex exemplars of carefully crafted works of literature. Close reading is used throughout the units to guide students toward revisiting the text and using textual evidence to respond to prompts orally and in writing. Students must analyze the story elements in multiple assignments for each section of the book. All of these strategies work together to rigorously guide students through their study of literature.

The next few pages will make clear how to use this guide for a purposeful and meaningful literature study. Each section of this guide is set up in the same way to make it easier for you to implement the instruction in your classroom.

Theme Thoughts

The great works of literature used throughout this series have important themes that have been relevant to people for many years. Many of the themes will be discussed during the various sections of this instructional guide. However, it would also benefit students to have independent time to think about the key themes of the novel.

Before students begin reading, have them complete *Pre-Reading Theme Thoughts* (page 13). This graphic organizer will allow students to think about the themes outside the context of the story. They'll have the opportunity to evaluate statements based on important themes and defend their opinions. Be sure to have students keep their papers for comparison to the *Post-Reading Theme Thoughts* (page 64). This graphic organizer is similar to the pre-reading activity. However, this time, students will be answering the questions from the point of view of one of the characters in the novel. They have to think about how the character would feel about each statement and defend their thoughts. To conclude the activity, have students compare what they thought about the themes before they read the novel to what the characters discovered during the story.

How to Use This Literature Guide (cont.)

Vocabulary

Each teacher overview page has definitions and sentences about how key vocabulary words are used in the section. These words should be introduced and discussed with students. There are two student vocabulary activity pages in each section. On the first page, students are asked to define the ten words chosen by the author of this unit. On the second page in most sections, each student will select at least eight words that he or she finds interesting or difficult. For each section, choose one of these pages for your students to complete. With either assignment, you may want to have students get into pairs to discuss the meanings of the words. Allow students to use reference guides to define the words. Monitor students to make sure the definitions they have found are accurate and relate to how the words are used in the text.

On some of the vocabulary student pages, students are asked to answer text-related questions about the vocabulary words. The following question stems will help you create your own vocabulary questions if you'd like to extend the discussion.

- How does this word describe _____'s character?
- In what ways does this word relate to the problem in this story?
- How does this word help you understand the setting?
- In what ways is this word related to the story's solution?
- Describe how this word supports the novel's theme of . . . .
- What visual images does this word bring to your mind?
- For what reasons might the author have chosen to use this particular word?

At times, more work with the words will help students understand their meanings. The following quick vocabulary activities are a good way to further study the words.

- Have students practice their vocabulary and writing skills by creating sentences and/or paragraphs in which multiple vocabulary words are used correctly and with evidence of understanding.
- Students can play vocabulary concentration. Students make a set of cards with the words and a separate set of cards with the definitions. Then, students lay the cards out on the table and play concentration. The goal of the game is to match vocabulary words with their definitions.
- Students can create word journal entries about the words. Students choose words they think are important and then describe why they think each word is important within the novel.

How to Use This Literature Guide (cont.)

Analyzing the Literature

After students have read each section, hold small-group or whole-class discussions. Questions are written at two levels of complexity to allow you to decide which questions best meet the needs of your students. The Level 1 questions are typically less abstract than the Level 2 questions. Level 1 is indicated by a square, while Level 2 is indicated by a triangle. These questions focus on the various story elements, such as character, setting, and plot. Student pages are provided if you want to assign these questions for individual student work before your group discussion. Be sure to add further questions as your students discuss what they've read. For each question, a few key points are provided for your reference as you discuss the novel with students.

Reader Response

In today's classrooms, there are often great readers who are below-average writers. So much time and energy is spent in classrooms getting students to read on grade level that little time is left to focus on writing skills. To help teachers include more writing in their daily literacy instruction, each section of this guide has a literature-based reader response prompt. Each of the three genres of writing is used in the reader responses within this guide: narrative, informative/explanatory, and argument. Students have a choice between two prompts for each reader response. One response requires students to make connections between the reading and their own lives. The other prompt requires students to determine text-to-text connections or connections within the text.

Close Reading the Literature

Within each section, students are asked to closely reread a short section of text. Since some versions of the novels have different page numbers, the selections are described by chapter and location, along with quotations to guide the readers. After each close reading, there are text-dependent questions to be answered by students.

Encourage students to read each question one at a time and then go back to the text and discover the answer. Work with students to ensure that they use the text to determine their answers rather than making unsupported inferences. Once students have answered the questions, discuss what they discovered. Suggested answers are provided in the answer key.

How to Use This Literature Guide (cont.)

Close Reading the Literature (cont.)

The generic, open-ended stems below can be used to write your own text-dependent questions if you would like to give students more practice.

- Give evidence from the text to support . . . .
- Justify your thinking using text evidence about . . . .
- Find evidence to support your conclusions about . . . .
- What text evidence helps the reader understand . . . ?
- Use the book to tell why _____ happens.
- Based on events in the story, ...
- Use text evidence to describe why . . . .

Making Connections

The activities in this section help students make cross-curricular connections to writing, mathematics, science, social studies, or the fine arts. Each of these types of activities requires higher-order thinking skills from students.

Creating with the Story Elements

It is important to spend time discussing the common story elements in literature. Understanding the characters, setting, and plot can increase students' comprehension and appreciation of the story. If teachers discuss these elements daily, students will more likely internalize the concepts and look for the elements in their independent reading. Another important reason for focusing on the story elements is that students will be better writers if they think about how the stories they read are constructed.

Students are given three options for working with the story elements. They are asked to create something related to the characters, setting, or plot of the novel. Students are given a choice in this activity so that they can decide to complete the activity that most appeals to them. Different multiple intelligences are used so that the activities are diverse and interesting to all students.

How to Use This Literature Guide (cont.)

Culminating Activity

This open-ended, cross-curricular activity requires higher-order thinking and allows for a creative product. Students will enjoy getting the chance to share what they have discovered through reading the novel. Be sure to allow them enough time to complete the activity at school or home.

Comprehension Assessment

The questions in this section are modeled after current standardized tests to help students analyze what they've read and prepare for tests they may see in their classrooms. The questions are dependent on the text and require critical-thinking skills to answer.

Response to Literature

The final post-reading activity is an essay based on the text that also requires further research by students. This is a great way to extend this book into other curricular areas. A suggested rubric is provided for teacher reference.

Correlation to the Standards

Shell Education is committed to producing educational materials that are research and standards based. As part of this effort, we have correlated all of our products to the academic standards of all 50 states, the District of Columbia, the Department of Defense Dependents Schools, and all Canadian provinces.

Purpose and Intent of Standards

Standards are designed to focus instruction and guide adoption of curricula. Standards are statements that describe the criteria necessary for students to meet specific academic goals. They define the knowledge, skills, and content students should acquire at each level. Standards are also used to develop standardized tests to evaluate students' academic progress. Teachers are required to demonstrate how their lessons meet standards. Standards are used in the development of all of our products, so educators can be assured they meet high academic standards.

How to Find Standards Correlations

To print a customized correlation report of this product for your state, visit our website at http://www.shelleducation.com and follow the online directions. If you require assistance in printing correlation reports, please contact our Customer Service Department at 1-877-777-3450.

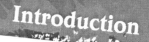

Correlation to the Standards (cont.)

Standards Correlation Chart

The lessons in this book were written to support today's college and career readiness standards. The following chart indicates which lessons address each standard.

College and Career Readiness Standard	Section
Read closely to determine what the text says explicitly and to make logical inferences from it; cite specific textual evidence when writing or speaking to support conclusions drawn from the text. (R.1)	Close Reading the Literature Sections 1–5
Determine central ideas or themes of a text and analyze their development; summarize the key supporting details and ideas. (R.2)	Analyzing the Literature Sections 1–5; Reader Response Sections 1–5; Response to Literature
Analyze how and why individuals, events, or ideas develop and interact over the course of a text. (R.3)	Analyzing the Literature Sections 1–5; Reader Response Sections 1–5; Response to Literature
Interpret words and phrases as they are used in a text, including determining technical, connotative, and figurative meanings, and analyze how specific word choices shape meaning or tone. (R.4)	Vocabulary Sections 1–5
Analyze the structure of texts, including how specific sentences, paragraphs, and larger portions of the text (e.g., a section, chapter, scene, or stanza) relate to each other and the whole. (R.5)	Making Connections Sections 1, 3, 5
Assess how point of view or purpose shapes the content and style of a text. (R.6)	Response to Literature
Read and comprehend complex literary and informational texts independently and proficiently. (R.10)	Entire Unit
Write arguments to support claims in an analysis of substantive topics or texts using valid reasoning and relevant and sufficient evidence. (W.1)	Reader Response Sections 1, 3–5
Write informative/explanatory texts to examine and convey complex ideas and information clearly and accurately through the effective selection, organization, and analysis of content. (W.2)	Reader Response Sections 1–4
Write narratives to develop real or imagined experiences or events using effective technique, well-chosen details, and well-structured event sequences. (W.3)	Reader Response Sections 2, 5
Produce clear and coherent writing in which the development, organization, and style are appropriate to task, purpose, and audience. (W.4)	Reader Response Sections 1–5
Conduct short as well as more sustained research projects based on focused questions, demonstrating understanding of the subject under investigation. (W.7)	Making Connections Section 2; Creating with the Story Elements Sections 3–4
Gather relevant information from multiple print and digital sources, assess the credibility and accuracy of each source, and integrate the information while avoiding plagiarism. (W.8)	Making Connections Section 2; Creating with the Story Elements Sections 3–4
Draw evidence from literary or informational texts to support analysis, reflection, and research. (W.9)	Close Reading the Literature Sections 1–5; Analyzing the Literature Sections 1–5

Correlation to the Standards (cont.)

Standards Correlation Chart (cont.)

College and Career Readiness Standard	Section
Prepare for and participate effectively in a range of conversations and collaborations with diverse partners, building on others' ideas and expressing their own clearly and persuasively. (SL.1)	Culminating Activity 1
Integrate and evaluate information presented in diverse media and formats, including visually, quantitatively, and orally. (SL.2)	Making Connections Section 2
Evaluate a speaker's point of view, reasoning, and use of evidence and rhetoric. (SL.3)	Analyzing the Literature Sections 1–5; Close Reading the Literature Sections 1–5
Present information, findings, and supporting evidence such that listeners can follow the line of reasoning and the organization, development, and style are appropriate to task, purpose, and audience. (SL.4)	Making Connections Section 2; Creating with the Story Elements Sections 3–4
Make strategic use of digital media and visual displays of data to express information and enhance understanding of presentations. (SL.5)	Creating with the Story Elements Sections 1–5
Demonstrate command of the conventions of standard English grammar and usage when writing or speaking. (L.1)	Reader Response Sections 1–5
Demonstrate command of the conventions of standard English capitalization, punctuation, and spelling when writing. (L.2)	Reader Response Sections 1–5
Apply knowledge of language to understand how language functions in different contexts, to make effective choices for meaning or style, and to comprehend more fully when reading or listening. (L.3)	Making Connections Sections 1, 3
Determine or clarify the meaning of unknown and multiple-meaning words and phrases by using context clues, analyzing meaningful word parts, and consulting general and specialized reference materials, as appropriate. (L.4)	Vocabulary Sections 1–5
Demonstrate understanding of figurative language, word relationships, and nuances in word meanings. (L.5)	Making Connections Sections 1, 3
Acquire and use accurately a range of general academic and domain-specific words and phrases sufficient for reading, writing, speaking, and listening at the college and career readiness level; demonstrate independence in gathering vocabulary knowledge when encountering an unknown term important to comprehension or expression. (L.6)	Vocabulary Words Sections 1–5

TESOL and WIDA Standards

The lessons in this book promote English language development for English language learners. The following TESOL and WIDA English Language Development Standards are addressed through the activities in this book:

- **Standard 1:** English language learners communicate for social and instructional purposes within the school setting.

- **Standard 2:** English language learners communicate information, ideas and concepts necessary for academic success in the content area of language arts.

About the Author—Zora Neale Hurston

Zora Neale Hurston was born in 1891 in Notasulga, Alabama. When she was three years old, Hurston's family moved to the rural township of Eatonville, Florida. This was a community located near Orlando that was populated and run entirely by African Americans. Hurston, her parents, and her seven brothers and sisters lived in an eight-room house on five acres of land.

Hurston's happy childhood ended abruptly with the death of her mother when she was thirteen. Hurston attended a boarding school for a time, but she was expelled for nonpayment of her tuition. She worked menial jobs, including as a maid and wardrobe girl for a traveling theater troupe. By age 26, Hurston was determined to pursue higher education, but she did not have a high school diploma. Too old to qualify for public assistance to finish high school, Hurston lied about her age on a high school application, pretending to be sixteen. In 1918, she received her high school diploma from the High School of Morgan College and began undergraduate studies at Howard University. Hurston received an associate's degree from Howard in 1920, and she was accepted into Barnard College, where she was the only African American student. Hurston graduated from Barnard College in 1928 with a bachelor of arts degree in anthropology. She then spent two years as a graduate student at Columbia University.

Hurston published her first novel, *Jonah's Gourd Vine*, in 1934. *Jonah's Gourd Vine* was followed by *Mules and Men* in 1935, a study of Southern African American oral traditions. *Their Eyes Were Watching God*, Hurston's most famous novel, was published in 1937. It was followed by *Tell My Horse* (1938), a study of voodoo practices and beliefs in Haiti and Jamaica, *Moses, Man of the Mountain* (1939), and *Dust Tracks on a Road* (1942), an autobiography. *Seraph on the Suwanee*, Hurston's final novel, was published in 1948.

Hurston married twice, but neither of the marriages lasted and she had no children. She was an important figure in the Harlem Renaissance movement and was the preeminent African American female author of her day. Yet Hurston was penniless when she died of hypertensive heart disease in 1960 at age 69. In the decades leading up to and following her death, her works were largely ignored. In 1973, the American novelist Alice Walker located Hurston's unmarked grave in a Florida cemetery and had a headstone placed there which reads: "Zora Neale Hurston: A Genius of the South." Walker also played an important role in re-popularizing Hurston's works. Today, *Their Eyes Were Watching God* is considered Hurston's masterwork and a classic of American literature.

Possible Texts for Text Comparisons

Bronx Masquerade by Nikki Grimes is a young adult novel in which contemporary high school students studying the Harlem Renaissance are inspired to begin writing poetry. *A Raisin in the Sun* by Lorraine Hansberry is a play set in Chicago in the mid-twentieth century. The plot revolves around issues of race, class, family ties, and choices involving self-sacrifice or risk-taking. *Coming of Age in Mississippi* by Anne Moody is an autobiographical account of the author's experiences growing up poor, black, and female in the American South of the mid-twentieth century.

Book Summary of *Their Eyes Were Watching God*

The novel opens with middle-aged Janie Starks returning to her home in Eatonville, Florida. As Janie tells her story to her friend, Pheoby, the narrative leaps back in time and Janie is sixteen, being raised by her grandmother, Nanny. Nanny sees Janie kiss a man and declares that it is time for Janie to be married. She explains that her desire to see Janie safely settled down is due to the fact that both Janie and her mother were the products of rape. Janie reluctantly agrees to marry a well-off, middle-aged farmer named Logan Killicks. Once married, she is deeply dissatisfied.

After Nanny dies, Janie abandons Killicks and runs off with an ambitious man named Joe Starks. The two marry and relocate to the new, all-black town of Eatonville. Janie works in the store, where locals entertain themselves with stories and banter, but Joe discourages her from participating in the fun and encourages her to remain silent. Joe becomes increasingly abusive toward Janie. As his health begins to suffer, he enlists the help of a folk healer, spreads the rumor that Janie has poisoned him, and refuses to allow her into his sick room. She finally gets to speak her mind, however, before Joe dies of kidney failure.

After Joe's death, Janie meets a younger, penniless man named Tea Cake. Janie travels to Jacksonville and marries him. Tea Cake persuades Janie to come with him to "the muck" near Lake Okeechobee, where a party atmosphere prevails with Tea Cake and Janie's house being the center of fun. Because they are enjoying life, Tea Cake and Janie choose to ignore hurricane warnings. However, when the hurricane causes the lake to rise, the couple is forced to flee on foot for higher ground. While escaping the hurricane, Tea Cake is bitten by a dog and contracts distemper. As his condition worsens, Tea Cake begins to suspect Janie of being unfaithful. When the crazed Tea Cake attempts to kill Janie, she is forced to shoot him in self-defense. She is put on trial for murder but is quickly acquitted. After providing Tea Cake with a splendid funeral, Janie returns home to her house in Eatonville, which is now filled with fond memories of Tea Cake.

Cross-Curricular Connection

This novel can be used in tandem with a social studies or visual arts unit on the Harlem Renaissance.

Possible Texts for Text Sets

- Campbell, Mary Schmidt. *Harlem Renaissance: Art of Black America*. Harry N. Abrams, 1994.
- Hill, Laban Carrick. *Harlem Stomp! A Cultural History of the Harlem Renaissance*. Little Brown, 2004.
- Koopmans, Andy. *The Harlem Renaissance*. Lucent, 2005.
- Rodgers, Marie. *The Harlem Renaissance: An Annotated Guide for Student Research*. Libraries Unlimited, 1998.

Name _____

Date _____

Pre-Reading Theme Thoughts

Directions: Read each of the statements in the first column. Decide if you agree or disagree with the statements. Record your opinion by marking an X in Agree or Disagree for each statement. Explain your choices in the fourth column. There are no right or wrong answers.

Statement	Agree	Disagree	Explain Your Answer
Physical comforts and financial security are not what make a person happy.			
A person who really loves you will want you to learn new things and express yourself.			
You can't live life by standing still. You have to set out on the road and take a risk.			
Envy is dangerous because it makes people believe the worst when they should know better.			

Vocabulary Overview

Ten key words from this section are provided below with definitions and sentences about how the words are used in the book. Choose one of the vocabulary activity sheets (pages 15 or 16) for students to complete as they read this section. Monitor students as they work to ensure the definitions they have found are accurate and relate to the text. Finally, discuss these important vocabulary words with students. If you think these words or other words in the section warrant more time devoted to them, there are suggestions in the introduction for other vocabulary activities (page 5).

Word	Definition	Sentence about Text
varicolored (ch. 1)	having a variety of colors	The sunset, made up of **varicolored** cloud dust, darkens as Janie talks and eats with Pheoby.
sanctum (ch. 2)	a sacred or holy place	The pear tree's blossom, visited by a bee, appears a holy **sanctum** to young Janie.
remorseless (ch. 2)	without pity or compassion	Janie feels a **remorseless** pain while contemplating the blossom and bee.
languid (ch. 2)	slow of movement; sluggish	Janie is limp and **languid** as she stares at the bee in the pear tree's blossoms.
shiftless (ch. 2)	showing a lack of ambition; laziness	Janie kisses a **shiftless** young man named Johnny Taylor.
lacerating (ch. 2)	tearing; wounding; mangling	To Nanny, the undesirable Johnny Taylor seems to be **lacerating** Janie with his kiss.
affirmation (ch. 2)	the assertion that something is true	Nanny nods in **affirmation** as she declares that Janie has now become a woman.
desecrating (ch. 2)	defiling; showing a lack of respect for something sacred	The idea of marrying Logan Killicks is **desecrating** Janie's vision of the bee and blossom.
conjecture (ch. 3)	a guess based on incomplete evidence	Janie makes the **conjecture** that she will begin to love Logan Killicks once she is married to him.
mien (ch. 3)	bearing or manner	Nanny keeps a stern **mien** as she tries to convince Janie that she will soon change her mind.

Name _____

Date _____

Understanding Vocabulary Words

Directions: The following words appear in this section of the book. Use context clues and reference materials to determine an accurate definition for each word.

Word	Definition
varicolored (ch. 1)	
sanctum (ch. 2)	
remorseless (ch. 2)	
languid (ch. 2)	
shiftless (ch. 2)	
lacerating (ch. 2)	
affirmation (ch. 2)	
desecrating (ch. 2)	
conjecture (ch. 3)	
mien (ch. 3)	

Name _____

Date _____

During-Reading Vocabulary Activity

Directions: As you read these chapters, record at least eight important words on the lines below. Try to find interesting, difficult, intriguing, special, or funny words. Your words can be long or short. They can be hard or easy to spell. After each word, use context clues in the text and reference materials to define the word.

- _____
- _____
- _____
- _____
- _____
- _____
- _____
- _____
- _____
- _____

Directions: Respond to these questions about the words in this section.

1. Which minor character is referred to as **shiftless**, and what does this tell us about him?

_____

_____

2. What are Janie's **conjectures** about how she will change once she's married?

_____

_____

Analyzing the Literature

Provided below are discussion questions you can use in small groups, with the whole class, or for written assignments. Each question is given at two levels so you can choose the right question for each group of students. Activity sheets with these questions are provided (pages 18–19) if you want students to write their responses. For each question, a few key discussion points are provided for your reference.

Story Element	■ Level 1	▲ Level 2	Key Discussion Points
Setting	How does young Janie see herself as similar to the pear tree she is lying under?	What does the pear tree symbolize to Janie? What feelings does it bring out in her?	Janie feels that she is in bloom, just like the tree. Students may note that the activity of the bees in the blossoms is a metaphor for sexual maturity. The vision of blossoming springtime makes Janie feel dreamy and almost under a spell. She wishes to share in the bliss that she associates with the blooming tree.
Character	Is Nanny doing a good or bad thing when she pushes Janie into marriage with Logan Killicks? Explain your answer.	What motivates Nanny to pressure Janie into the marriage with Logan Killicks? Do you sympathize with her desire to see Janie married?	Nanny sees this marriage as "protection." Her primary goal is to see Janie "safe in life," in a situation where no man will "make a spit cup" out of her. Students may say that while they sympathize with Nanny's fears, forcing a young person into an empty marriage is unfair. Janie deserves the chance to experience love.
Character	What do you think Janie's future with Logan would have been like based on his decision to purchase the new mule?	How does Logan's decision to purchase a new mule represent a turning point in his relationship with Janie?	The purchase of the mule suggests that in the future Janie would be forced to do hard labor. Logan has become frustrated and angry with Janie because she does not love, respect, or desire him. His pride is hurt because he sees that the marriage is unequal, and he now wishes to make Janie suffer for that inequality.
Plot	Should Janie have run off with Joe Starks? Why or why not?	How do you predict things will go for Joe and Janie? Has she made a good or bad choice? What makes you think so?	Students may sympathize with Janie's decision to get away before she is forced into hard labor. Because Joe seems ambitious, students may feel that Janie will have a bright future with him. Others may note that Joe does "not represent sun-up and pollen and blooming trees," and they may predict that Janie will still feel unfulfilled with him.

Name _____

Date _____

Analyzing the Literature

Directions: Think about the section you just read. Read each question and state your response with textual evidence.

1. How does young Janie see herself as similar to the pear tree she is lying under?

_____

_____

_____

_____

2. Is Nanny doing a good or bad thing when she pushes Janie into marriage with Logan Killicks? Explain your answer.

_____

_____

_____

_____

3. What do you think Janie's future with Logan would have been like based on his decision to purchase the new mule?

_____

_____

_____

4. Should Janie have run off with Joe Starks? Why or why not?

_____

_____

_____

Name _____

Date _____

▲ Analyzing the Literature

Directions: Think about the section you just read. Read each question and state your response with textual evidence.

1. What does the pear tree symbolize to Janie? What feelings does it bring out in her?

_____

_____

_____

_____

2. What motivates Nanny to pressure Janie into the marriage with Logan Killicks? Do you sympathize with her desire to see Janie married?

_____

_____

_____

_____

3. How does Logan's decision to purchase a new mule represent a turning point in his relationship with Janie?

_____

_____

_____

4. How do you predict things will go for Joe and Janie? Has she made a good or bad choice? What makes you think so?

_____

_____

_____

Name _____

Date _____

Reader Response

Directions: Choose one of the following prompts about this section to answer. Be sure you include a topic sentence in your response, use textual evidence to support your opinion, and provide a strong conclusion that summarizes your opinion.

Writing Prompts

- **Informative/Explanatory Piece**—What is Nanny's view of marriage, and how is it different from Janie's? What is your own view of marriage? Is it more similar to Nanny's view or Janie's view?

- **Argument Piece**—Nanny says that "you can't beat nobody down so low" that you "rob [them] of [their] will." She argues that people are always free in a sense because they are free to wish for something better. Use evidence from the novel to explain why you agree or disagree with Nanny.

_____

_____

_____

_____

_____

_____

_____

_____

_____

_____

_____

Name _____

Date _____

Close Reading the Literature

Directions: Closely reread the pages in chapter 4 where Joe Starks is introduced. Stop with, ". . . to rest a week or two." Read each question and then revisit the text to find evidence that supports your answer.

1. List at least three specific details about Joe Starks's clothing and appearance. Why are these details significant? What do they tell Janie (and the reader) about Joe?

   _____

   _____

   _____

2. Where is Joe going and what does he hope to do when he gets there? Support your answer with evidence from the text.

   _____

   _____

   _____

3. What doesn't Joe "represent" to Janie, according to the text? What does he "speak for" instead?

   _____

   _____

   _____

4. Based on what has happened so far, why is Janie drawn to Joe Starks?

   _____

   _____

   _____

Name _____

Date _____

Making Connections–Dialogue in Dialect

Zora Neale Hurston was not just a novelist but also a student of anthropology. She was deeply interested in linguistic anthropology, which is the study of speech patterns and the relationship between communication and culture. The novel reflects her interest in dialects and speech patterns. In the novel, Hurston's characters speak in a dialect, frequently expressing themselves through the use of inventive figures of speech, such as similes, metaphors, and hyperbole.

Directions: The following sentences from chapters 1–4 are written in dialect and contain figures of speech. Translate each phrase into standard, contemporary English that expresses its meaning.

1. Janie: "I reckon they got me up in they mouth now." (ch. 1)

_____

_____

2. Nanny: "Look lak she been livin' through uh hundred years in January without one day of spring." (ch. 2)

_____

_____

_____

3. Nanny: "What you come in heah wid uh face long as mah arm for?" (ch. 3)

_____

_____

4. Joe: "Janie, if you think Ah aims to tole you off and make a dog outa you, youse wrong." (ch. 4)

_____

_____

Name _____

Date _____

Creating with the Story Elements

Directions: Thinking about the story elements of character, setting, and plot in a novel is very important to understanding what is happening and why. Complete **one** of the following activities based on what you've read so far. Be creative and have fun!

Characters

Pretend that you have been given the task of turning *Their Eyes Were Watching God* into a musical or a movie with a soundtrack. Assign a signature song to each of the major characters featured in the first four chapters of the novel. Write an explanation of why you selected each song.

Setting

The pear tree and the road are physical elements that play an important role in the first four chapters of *Their Eyes Were Watching God*. Create a painting, drawing, or collage that explores the significance and symbolism of either the tree or the road. Be ready to present your artwork to the class, explaining why you included specific images and elements.

Plot

Write each important event that happens (or that we learn about) in the first four chapters on an index card or slip of paper. On a larger piece of paper or poster board, assemble the index cards or slips of paper into a flow chart, using arrows to show cause and effect. Then, use your chart to make predictions about what might happen next.

Vocabulary Overview

Ten key words from this section are provided below with definitions and sentences about how the words are used in the book. Choose one of the vocabulary activity sheets (pages 25 or 26) for students to complete as they read this section. Monitor students as they work to ensure the definitions they have found are accurate and relate to the text. Finally, discuss these important vocabulary words with students. If you think these words or other words in the section warrant more time devoted to them, there are suggestions in the introduction for other vocabulary activities (page 5).

Word	Definition	Sentence about Text
temerity (ch. 5)	extreme confidence or boldness	None of the townspeople have the **temerity** to challenge Joe.
figuratively (ch. 6)	not literally, but metaphorically	The men of the town enjoy **figuratively** wallowing in Janie's long, pretty hair.
orator (ch. 6)	someone skilled at public speaking	When Janie finally speaks up, one of the men comments on her talent as an **orator**.
hammock (ch. 6)	a fertile, treed area higher than its surroundings	The men drag the dead mule to the edge of the **hammock**.
eulogy (ch. 6)	a speech praising someone who has just died	Joe gives a **eulogy** to honor the dead mule.
distended (ch. 6)	swollen; bloated	Joe delivers the speech while standing on the **distended** stomach of the mule.
coquetry (ch. 6)	flirtatiousness	Despite her age, Mrs. Bogle has an air of **coquetry** about her.
dudgeon (ch. 6)	a feeling of offense or resentment	Mrs. Tony is said to be in a state of high **dudgeon** after Joe gives her only a small piece of meat.
stolidness (ch. 7)	the condition of being unemotional and difficult to stir up	After years of putting up with Joe, Janie develops **stolidness**.
pugnaciously (ch. 7)	showing a readiness or desire to fight or argue	Joe's belly thrusts out **pugnaciously**.

Name _____

Date _____

Understanding Vocabulary Words

Directions: The following words appear in this section of the book. Use context clues and reference materials to determine an accurate definition for each word.

Word	Definition
temerity (ch. 5)	
figuratively (ch. 6)	
orator (ch. 6)	
hammock (ch. 6)	
eulogy (ch. 6)	
distended (ch. 6)	
coquetry (ch. 6)	
dudgeon (ch. 6)	
stolidness (ch. 7)	
pugnaciously (ch. 7)	

Name _____

Date _____

During-Reading Vocabulary Activity

Directions: As you read these chapters, record at least eight important words on the lines below. Try to find interesting, difficult, intriguing, special, or funny words. Your words can be long or short. They can be hard or easy to spell. After each word, use context clues in the text and reference materials to define the word.

- _____
- _____
- _____
- _____
- _____
- _____
- _____
- _____
- _____
- _____

Directions: Respond to these questions about the words in this section.

1. Why are the townspeople surprised that Janie has skill as an **orator**?

_____

_____

2. How might a person with **stolidness** respond to an insult or compliment?

_____

_____

_____

Analyzing the Literature

Provided below are discussion questions you can use in small groups, with the whole class, or for written assignments. Each question is given at two levels so you can choose the right question for each group of students. Activity sheets with these questions are provided (pages 28–29) if you want students to write their responses. For each question, a few key discussion points are provided for your reference.

Story Element	■ Level 1	▲ Level 2	Key Discussion Points
Setting	What are some of the changes that Joe makes to Eatonville after he and Janie move there? Why does he make these changes?	Is Eatonville better off because of the changes that Joe makes to the town? What motivates him to make these changes?	Joe builds a store, organizes the building of roads, puts up a streetlight, opens a post office, and builds a "big house" to live in. Students may argue that the town is now better off. However, Joe is motivated by ambition. He wants to be king of a better kingdom.
Character	Find a passage in the text where Janie remains silent. What might happen if she spoke up instead?	Locate passages in the text where Janie is silent or silenced. What motivates her to remain silent? What impact does this silence have on her life?	Janie is forced to remain silent instead of giving a speech in chapter 5. The townspeople comment on her silence in this same chapter. In chapter 6, we learn that Joe has forbidden her to tell stories on the porch. He tells her that she is "too moufy." The silence is intended to pacify Joe, but it separates her from the rest of the people. Silent, she becomes a powerless ornament.
Character	Why does Janie feel isolated and unhappy in Eatonville?	How do the townspeople view Janie? How does Janie feel about her relationship with the townspeople?	The townspeople view her with "awe" and "envy" because of her position as Mrs. Mayor. Janie feels separated and excluded because of the class difference, unable to "get close" to the others. Joe reinforces the separation when he bans Janie from participating in the conversation on the store porch and keeps her from attending the mule funeral in chapter 6.
Plot	What do you think will happen next to Janie and Joe? What makes you think so?	Predict what will happen next to Janie and Joe. Point to details in chapter 7 that seem to foreshadow their future.	Students may predict the further breakdown or break up of the marriage based on the fact that Janie has finally spoken up and defended herself and a humiliated Joe has struck Janie in chapter 7. Some students may note Joe's poor health and may predict it will worsen and come into play in later pages.

Name _____

Date _____

Analyzing the Literature

Directions: Think about the section you just read. Read each question and state your response with textual evidence.

1. What are some of the changes that Joe makes to Eatonville after he and Janie move there? Why does he make these changes?

_____

_____

_____

_____

2. Find a passage in the text where Janie remains silent. What might happen if she spoke up instead?

_____

_____

_____

_____

3. Why does Janie feel isolated and unhappy in Eatonville?

_____

_____

_____

_____

4. What do you think will happen next to Janie and Joe? What makes you think so?

_____

_____

_____

Name _____

Date _____

▲ Analyzing the Literature

Directions: Think about the section you just read. Read each question and state your response with textual evidence.

1. Is Eatonville better off because of the changes that Joe makes to the town? What motivates him to make these changes?

   _____

   _____

   _____

   _____

2. Locate passages in the text where Janie is silent or silenced. What motivates her to remain silent? What impact does this silence have on her life?

   _____

   _____

   _____

   _____

3. How do the townspeople view Janie? How does Janie feel about her relationship with the townspeople?

   _____

   _____

   _____

4. Predict what will happen next to Janie and Joe. Point to details in chapter 7 that seem to foreshadow their future.

   _____

   _____

   _____

Name _____

Date _____

Reader Response

Directions: Choose one of the following prompts about this section to answer. Be sure you include a topic sentence in your response, use textual evidence to support your opinion, and provide a strong conclusion that summarizes your opinion.

Writing Prompts

- **Informative/Explanatory Piece**—How does the store serve as a sort of community center for the town of Eatonville? Describe a place in your own home, school, or neighborhood that serves a similar function. Who gathers there? What do these community members do for entertainment?

- **Narrative Piece**—In *Their Eyes Were Watching God*, the townspeople amuse themselves by making up stories about Matt Bonner's mule. Explain which of the mule stories is your favorite and why.

_____

_____

_____

_____

_____

_____

_____

_____

_____

_____

_____

_____

_____

_____

Name _____

Date _____

Close Reading the Literature

Directions: Closely reread the first few pages of chapter 7. Read each question and then revisit the text to find evidence that supports your answer.

1. Find the sentences where a road is mentioned in the first and second paragraphs of this passage. How does the road serve as a metaphor in these two paragraphs?

   _____

   _____

   _____

2. In paragraph four, what doesn't Janie realize about herself due to the fact that she doesn't "read books"?

   _____

   _____

   _____

3. The text describes how Janie splits herself mentally into two separate parts. What are the separate parts doing in the description here?

   _____

   _____

   _____

4. Why does Joe begin talking about Janie's age all the time? Support your answer with evidence from the text.

   _____

   _____

   _____

Name _____

Date _____

Making Connections–The Harlem Renaissance

Zora Neale Hurston is often associated with the Harlem Renaissance. This was a rich period of growth in African American arts and culture, which spanned approximately from the late 1910s to the mid-1930s. Harlem, a primarily African American neighborhood of New York City, was a main center of the movement. During this period, art forms that had their origin in African American culture, such as blues and jazz music, were embraced by the larger public. African American figures rose to national and international prominence in fields such as literature, theater, opera, and classical music composition.

Directions: Select one of the Harlem Renaissance figures listed below. Using the library or Internet, research the life and accomplishments of your selected figure. Be ready to make a brief presentation of what you have learned. Include visual or auditory elements in your presentation.

Alain Locke	Jessie Fauset
Billie Holliday	Josephine Baker
Cab Calloway	Langston Hughes
Claude McKay	Lena Horne
Duke Ellington	Louis Armstrong
Eulalie Spence	Ma Rainey
Fats Waller	Marcus Garvey
James Baldwin	Marian Anderson
James Weldon Johnson	Paul Robeson
Jean Toomer	W.E.B. DuBois
"Jelly Roll" Morton	Willie "The Lion" Smith

Creating with the Story Elements

Directions: Thinking about the story elements of character, setting, and plot in a novel is very important to understanding what is happening and why. Complete **one** of the following activities based on what you've read so far. Be creative and have fun!

Characters

What if the characters in *Their Eyes Were Watching God* could participate in social media? Select a character and create a series of posts or tweets from that character's perspective.

Setting

Design a map of Eatonville as you imagine it. Include locations and objects mentioned in the novel, such as the store, the post office, the streetlamp, the "big house," and so forth.

Plot

Create a chart or poster that explores the different conflicts that are present in chapters 5–7 of *Their Eyes Were Watching God*. Use separate columns or color coding to distinguish internal from external conflicts. Be sure to include examples of both.

Vocabulary Overview

Ten key words from this section are provided below with definitions and sentences about how the words are used in the book. Choose one of the vocabulary activity sheets (pages 35 or 36) for students to complete as they read this section. Monitor students as they work to ensure the definitions they have found are accurate and relate to the text. Finally, discuss these important vocabulary words with students. If you think these words or other words in the section warrant more time devoted to them, there are suggestions in the introduction for other vocabulary activities (page 5).

Word	Definition	Sentence about Text
variance (ch. 8)	the state of being in disagreement	Pheoby comments that Janie and Joe have been at **variance** with one another.
menial (ch. 8)	humble; lowly; appropriate to a servant	People who used to go to the mayor's house only to do **menial** jobs now visit as Joe's confidants.
ostentatiously (ch. 8)	in a way that is meant to attract attention	The people checking up on Janie for Joe **ostentatiously** watch her in the store.
pacify (ch. 8)	to soothe; to make tranquil	Janie tells Joe that he should have made an effort to **pacify** others and not just himself.
globules (ch. 8)	tiny globes or balls of a liquid	Janie notices the sweat **globules** on Joe's face as he lies in bed dying.
insinuation (ch. 9)	a suggestion or implication	There is an **insinuation** of power in the clothing and vehicles of some people attending Joe's funeral.
refracted (ch. 9)	bounced off and changed directions	The attention of Janie's new suitors is **refracted** by her lack of interest.
scimitar (ch. 10)	a sword with a curved blade	Tea Cake's curved eyelashes look like **scimitars**.
transfiguration (ch. 11)	a complete change of appearance to a more beautiful or spiritual state	Janie's face undergoes a **transfiguration** when Tea Cake confesses his feelings for her.
excruciating (ch. 11)	unbearably painful	Janie finds her feelings of doubt **excruciating**.

Name _____

Date _____

Understanding Vocabulary Words

Directions: The following words appear in this section of the book. Use context clues and reference materials to determine an accurate definition for each word.

Word	Definition
variance (ch. 8)	
menial (ch. 8)	
ostentatiously (ch. 8)	
pacify (ch. 8)	
globules (ch. 8)	
insinuation (ch. 9)	
refracted (ch. 9)	
scimitar (ch. 10)	
transfiguration (ch. 11)	
excruciating (ch. 11)	

Name _____

Date _____

During-Reading Vocabulary Activity

Directions: As you read these chapters, record at least eight important words on the lines below. Try to find interesting, difficult, intriguing, special, or funny words. Your words can be long or short. They can be hard or easy to spell. After each word, use context clues in the text and reference materials to define the word.

- _____
- _____
- _____
- _____
- _____
- _____
- _____
- _____
- _____
- _____

Directions: Now, organize your words. Rewrite each of the words on a sticky note. Work with a group to create a bar graph of your words. Stack any words that are the same on top of one another. Different words should appear in different columns. Finally, discuss with the group why certain words were chosen more often than other words.

Analyzing the Literature

Provided below are discussion questions you can use in small groups, with the whole class, or for written assignments. Each question is given at two levels so you can choose the right question for each group of students. Activity sheets with these questions are provided (pages 38–39) if you want students to write their responses. For each question, a few key discussion points are provided for your reference.

Story Element	■ Level 1	▲ Level 2	Key Discussion Points
Character	What one change to her appearance does Janie make immediately after Joe dies? Why does she make this change?	What is the significance of Janie's decision to uncover her hair and burn her head rags?	Janie burns the head rags and begins wearing her hair down in a long braid. Students may see this as a sign of liberation. She is no longer forced to hide her true self and her beauty from others. She can now relax and "let her hair down" for a change.
Character	What can we tell about Tea Cake from the fact that he teaches Janie how to play checkers? How is Tea Cake different from Joe in this regard?	What is the significance of Tea Cake's decision to teach Janie checkers? How does he treat her as she is learning, and why is this important?	Tea Cake compliments Janie, saying she "looks hard to beat," then teaches her to play. Joe, on the other hand, kept her from trying, telling her she was too stupid to learn. Tea Cake jumps Janie's king when he can, giving her no special beginner privileges and instead treating her like an equal.
Setting	How does life at the house and store change with Tea Cake in the picture?	How does Tea Cake's presence change the atmosphere of the store and of the house? What physical changes does he make to the house and why are they significant?	Students may say that the store and house are more cheerful or seem to finally be Janie's, since she can now do what she likes, express herself, and enjoy herself in both places. Tea Cake makes flower beds for Janie and seeds the garden at her house. Students can be prompted to see a connection between Tea Cake's gardening and the pear tree of the novel's early chapters.
Plot	What are some new places that Janie goes with Tea Cake? Where do you think they might go next and why?	In chapter 8, Janie says that she feels "stone dead from standing still and trying to smile." How does Tea Cake help her to get moving again?	Tea Cake takes Janie to a picnic, to the movies in Orlando, to a baseball game, hunting, and fishing. He also gets a car and teaches her to drive. Students may predict that Janie and Tea Cake will leave Eatonville and embark on a greater adventure in coming chapters.

Name _____

Date _____

Analyzing the Literature

Directions: Think about the section you just read. Read each question and state your response with textual evidence.

1. What one change to her appearance does Janie make immediately after Joe dies? Why does she make this change?

_____

_____

_____

_____

2. What can we tell about Tea Cake from the fact that he teaches Janie how to play checkers? How is Tea Cake different from Joe in this regard?

_____

_____

_____

_____

3. How does life at the house and store change with Tea Cake in the picture?

_____

_____

_____

_____

4. What are some new places that Janie goes with Tea Cake? Where do you think they might go next and why?

_____

_____

_____

_____

Name _____

Date _____

▲ Analyzing the Literature

Directions: Think about the section you just read. Read each question and state your response with textual evidence.

1. What is the significance of Janie's decision to uncover her hair and burn her head rags?

   _____

   _____

   _____

   _____

2. What is the significance of Tea Cake's decision to teach Janie checkers? How does he treat her as she is learning, and why is this important?

   _____

   _____

   _____

   _____

3. How does Tea Cake's presence change the atmosphere of the store and of the house? What physical changes does he make to the house and why are they significant?

   _____

   _____

   _____

   _____

4. In chapter 8, Janie says that she feels "stone dead from standing still and trying to smile." How does Tea Cake help her to get moving again?

   _____

   _____

   _____

Name _____

Date _____

Reader Response

Directions: Choose one of the following prompts about this section to answer. Be sure you include a topic sentence in your response, use textual evidence to support your opinion, and provide a strong conclusion that summarizes your opinion.

Writing Prompts

- **Informative/Explanatory Piece**—Janie is angry at her grandmother for "tak[ing] the biggest thing God ever made, the horizon," and "pinch[ing] it into such a little bit of a thing that she could tie it about her granddaughter's neck tight enough to choke her." Compare Tea Cake to someone in your own life who helped you to "broaden your horizons" in some way.
- **Argument Piece**—The townspeople believe that Tea Cake is a poor match for Janie and that she is making a mistake in taking up with him. Do you agree? Explain your opinion.

_____

_____

_____

_____

_____

_____

_____

_____

_____

_____

_____

_____

Close Reading the Literature

Directions: Closely reread the first few pages of chapter 9. Read each question and then revisit the text to find evidence that supports your answer.

1. What does Janie look like on the outside during Joe's funeral? How does her outer appearance contrast with what is going on inside her during this time?

   _____

   _____

   _____

2. The house is personified in this passage and described as almost a double of Janie. What specific emotions and actions are attributed to the house?

   _____

   _____

   _____

3. Why doesn't Janie choose to "go back to where she had come from" and "look over the old stamping ground"? Cite the text to support your answer.

   _____

   _____

   _____

4. Janie thinks of life as a "journey to the horizons." What does she think she should have been searching for on this journey?

   _____

   _____

   _____

Name _____

Date _____

Making Connections–Personification in *Their Eyes Were Watching God*

A literary device that Hurston uses frequently in *Their Eyes Were Watching God* is personification. Personification is the attribution of human (or sometimes animal) characteristics to something inanimate. The author may describe the inanimate thing as having feelings, motives, an ability to speak, or otherwise behaving in human ways. A personified object or concept may be described as having body parts such as eyes, a face, arms, or legs.

Examples of personification:

- The sun touched her cheek with its gentle fingers.
- The rustling trees seemed to be whispering secrets to one another.

Directions: Reread the passage in chapter 8 of *Their Eyes Were Watching God* beginning with the words, "So Janie began to think of Death." Then read through the paragraph beginning with, "He was lying on his side. . . ." Find three examples of personification and describe them below.

Personified Object, Concept, or Force of Nature	Human Qualities

Name _____

Date _____

Creating with the Story Elements

Directions: Thinking about the story elements of character, setting, and plot in a novel is very important to understanding what is happening and why. Complete **one** of the following activities based on what you've read so far. Be creative and have fun!

Characters

Create a Venn diagram, collage, or other visual representation expressing the similarities and differences between the external Janie and the internal Janie and between Janie as others see her and Janie as she sees herself.

Setting

Using the Internet or library, research the real town of Eatonville, Florida. Locate photographs of the town, past and present, and display them on a poster, in a photo album or scrapbook, or as part of a digital presentation. Include photo captions with your display. Compare the real town to the town in the story.

Plot

Select a scene from chapters 8–12. Adapt the scene into a script for a movie, play, or radio show. Keep the dialogue in dialect, if you wish, or change the dialogue into contemporary language.

Vocabulary Overview

Ten key words from this section are provided below with definitions and sentences about how the words are used in the book. Choose one of the vocabulary activity sheets (pages 45 or 46) for students to complete as they read this section. Monitor students as they work to ensure the definitions they have found are accurate and relate to the text. Finally, discuss these important vocabulary words with students. If you think these words or other words in the section warrant more time devoted to them, there are suggestions in the introduction for other vocabulary activities (page 5).

Word	Definition	Sentence about Text
jook (ch. 14)	a bar featuring music and dancing	Practicing shooting and going to **jooks** are two things the people on the muck do for fun.
phosphorescent (ch. 14)	having a luminous, glowing appearance	Janie and Tea Cake hunt alligators by looking for their **phosphorescent** eyes in the dark.
transients (ch. 14)	people who stay only a short time in one place	The people who come to work on the muck are **transients**.
flivvers (ch. 14)	automobiles, especially inexpensive and old ones	The migrant workers arrive in **flivvers** with their dogs and families.
affront (ch. 16)	an offense to one's dignity and self-respect	The prejudiced Mrs. Turner sees very dark skin as an **affront**.
sacrilege (ch. 16)	the violation of anything held sacred	The things Mrs. Turner says about Booker T. Washington sound like **sacrilege** to Janie.
insensate (ch. 16)	cold, cruel, without human feeling or sensitivity	Mrs. Turner bows down to some people and treats others with **insensate** cruelty.
indiscriminate (ch. 16)	affecting or harming in a careless or unfair way	Mrs. Turner has seen **indiscriminate** suffering and so has come to believe that gods want people to suffer.
transmutation (ch. 16)	a change from one substance or form to another	Mrs. Turner experiences **transmutation** and feels herself to be "whiter" when around Janie.
defilement (ch. 16)	to make foul, dirty, or unclean	Mrs. Turner thinks of marriage to Tea Cake as a **defilement** of Janie.

Name _____

Date _____

Understanding Vocabulary Words

Directions: The following words appear in this section of the book. Use context clues and reference materials to determine an accurate definition for each word.

Word	Definition
jook (ch. 14)	
phosphorescent (ch. 14)	
transients (ch. 14)	
flivvers (ch. 14)	
affront (ch. 16)	
sacrilege (ch. 16)	
insensate (ch. 16)	
indiscriminate (ch. 16)	
transmutation (ch. 16)	
defilement (ch. 16)	

Name _____

Date _____

During-Reading Vocabulary Activity

Directions: As you read these chapters, record at least eight important words on the lines below. Try to find interesting, difficult, intriguing, special, or funny words. Your words can be long or short. They can be hard or easy to spell. After each word, use context clues in the text and reference materials to define the word.

- _____
- _____
- _____
- _____
- _____
- _____
- _____
- _____
- _____
- _____

Directions: Respond to these questions about the words in this section.

1. What might a person see or do at a **jook**?

_____

_____

2. What are the characteristics of someone who is a **transient**?

_____

_____

Analyzing the Literature

Provided below are discussion questions you can use in small groups, with the whole class, or for written assignments. Each question is given at two levels so you can choose the right question for each group of students. Activity sheets with these questions are provided (pages 48–49) if you want students to write their responses. For each question, a few key discussion points are provided for your reference.

Story Element	■ Level 1	▲ Level 2	Key Discussion Points
Character	Why does Mrs. Turner want to befriend Janie? Should Janie be friends with Mrs. Turner? Why or why not?	What are Mrs. Turner's prejudices, and what motivates her to try to befriend Janie? How should Janie respond to her overtures of friendship?	Mrs. Turner, described at length in chapter 16, is a lighter-skinned black woman who is prejudiced against those with darker skin. She admires Janie solely due to her "Caucasian characteristics." Students may or may not argue that Janie should try harder to break off relations with Mrs. Turner.
Plot	What events cause Janie and Tea Cake to become jealous, and how do they act when they're jealous? Should they act differently?	Describe times when Tea Cake and Janie get jealous. Do these jealousies serve to strengthen or weaken their relationship?	Nunkie flirts with Tea Cake in the fields in chapter 15, causing Janie to become jealous. Tea Cake becomes jealous when Mrs. Turner introduces her brother and suggests him as a more appropriate mate for Janie in chapter 16. The jealousy causes Tea Cake to strike Janie in chapter 17, though she forgives him.
Setting	How is life on the muck different from life as described in Eatonville?	Compare and contrast the environment and lifestyle of the people on the muck with the environment and lifestyle in Eatonville.	Students may respond that the muck environment seems wilder, rougher, rowdier, dirtier, or more relaxed and casual. They may point to the description of the fight in chapter 17 or of the parties at the house, events that aren't described in the Eatonville chapters. Similarities might include poverty in both places, the importance of storytelling in both locales, and so forth.
Character	How does Janie change or grow in these chapters?	Argue that Janie is either growing or regressing. Support your argument with details from the text.	At the end of chapter 13, we are told that Janie's soul has "crawled out from its hiding place." She has many new experiences, including learning to shoot and hunt and to work in the fields. She now feels free to laugh and talk and can tell "big stories herself."

Name _____

Date _____

■ Analyzing the Literature

Directions: Think about the section you just read. Read each question and state your response with textual evidence.

1. Why does Mrs. Turner want to befriend Janie? Should Janie be friends with Mrs. Turner? Why or why not?

_____

_____

_____

2. What events cause Janie and Tea Cake to become jealous, and how do they act when they're jealous? Should they act differently?

_____

_____

_____

_____

3. How is life on the muck different from life as described in Eatonville?

_____

_____

_____

_____

4. How does Janie change or grow in these chapters?

_____

_____

_____

_____

Name _____

Date _____

▲ Analyzing the Literature

Directions: Think about the section you just read. Read each question and state your response with textual evidence.

1. What are Mrs. Turner's prejudices, and what motivates her to try to befriend Janie? How should Janie respond to her overtures of friendship?

   _____

   _____

   _____

2. Describe times when Tea Cake and Janie get jealous. Do these jealousies serve to strengthen or weaken their relationship?

   _____

   _____

   _____

3. Compare and contrast the environment and lifestyle of the people on the muck with the environment and lifestyle in Eatonville.

   _____

   _____

   _____

4. Argue that Janie is either growing or regressing. Support your argument with details from the text.

   _____

   _____

   _____

   _____

Name _____

Date _____

Reader Response

Directions: Choose one of the following prompts about this section to answer. Be sure you include a topic sentence in your response, use textual evidence to support your opinion, and provide a strong conclusion that summarizes your opinion.

Writing Prompts

- **Argument Piece**—Is Tea Cake wrong to take Janie's money and spend it as he does? Is Janie right or wrong to forgive him so quickly? Describe a time when somebody "borrowed" money or something else from you without asking. How did you feel toward that person, and were you as quick to forgive as Janie?

- **Informative/Explanatory Piece**—Compare and contrast Janie's relationship with Tea Cake to her past relationship with Joe. What has changed for Janie in her new marriage, and what, if any, aspects of marriage remain the same?

_____

_____

_____

_____

_____

_____

_____

_____

_____

_____

_____

_____

Name _____

Date _____

Close Reading the Literature

Directions: Closely reread the first several pages of chapter 14. Stop at the paragraph where Janie is described picking beans. Read each question and then revisit the text to find evidence that supports your answer.

1. What new skill does Tea Cake teach Janie? Why does he think Janie should gain this skill? How does she feel about learning it?

_____

_____

_____

2. Why do people like to gather at Tea Cake and Janie's house? What is the attraction? Support your answer with direct references from the novel.

_____

_____

_____

3. Based on the novel, why does Janie begin working in the fields with Tea Cake? How does she feel about it?

_____

_____

_____

4. Why do the others on the muck see Janie as a "special case"? What makes them change their minds about her?

_____

_____

_____

Name _____

Date _____

Making Connections–Text to Self, Text to Text, Text to World

Directions: Consider the events in chapters 13–17 of *Their Eyes Were Watching God*. Read the questions below. Then, select one prompt and answer it on the lines provided. Use examples from the text to support your answer.

Text to Self—Explain how something that you've read in chapters 13–17 of *Their Eyes Were Watching God* relates to your own life.

Text to Text—Think of a book or article you've read or a non-print medium such as a film or TV program you've seen. Explain how this print or non-print medium relates to chapters 13–17 of *Their Eyes Were Watching God*.

Text to World—Describe something that has recently happened or is currently happening in your community, your country, or the world. Explain how this event connects to what you've just read in chapters 13–17 of Hurston's novel.

_____

_____

_____

_____

_____

_____

_____

_____

_____

_____

Creating with the Story Elements

Directions: Thinking about the story elements of character, setting, and plot in a novel is very important to understanding what is happening and why. Complete **one** of the following activities based on what you've read so far. Be creative and have fun!

Characters

Create two or more decorative postcards from the Everglades. Pretend to be Janie, Tea Cake, Mrs. Turner, or another character as you address and write the cards.

Setting

Research the Everglades using the library or Internet. Create a poster or digital presentation based on what you learn. Present information about the various groups of people who have lived in and around the area, including migrant farm workers.

Plot

Create a comic strip detailing the chain of events in Tea Cake's adventure with Janie's two hundred dollars.

Vocabulary Overview

Ten key words from this section are provided below with definitions and sentences about how the words are used in the book. Choose one of the vocabulary activity sheets (pages 55 or 56) for students to complete as they read this section. Monitor students as they work to ensure the definitions they have found are accurate and relate to the text. Finally, discuss these important vocabulary words with students. If you think these words or other words in the section warrant more time devoted to them, there are suggestions in the introduction for other vocabulary activities (page 5).

Word	Definition	Sentence about Text
subtleties (ch. 18)	complexity; fineness or carefulness	Janie enjoys listening to the **subtleties** of Stew Beef's drumming.
grotesques (ch. 18)	sculptures featuring mixed or distorted human and animal forms	The people dancing to Stew Beef's drumming look like living **grotesques**.
oblique (ch. 18)	not straight or direct	Janie grabs on to the cow that is swimming in an **oblique** line.
hackles (ch. 18)	hair standing up on the back of an animal's neck	The rabid dog is growling and has its **hackles** raised.
disgorged (ch. 19)	ejected or thrown out from the mouth or stomach	Although Tea Cake tries to swallow, the water keeps getting **disgorged** from his mouth.
supplication (ch. 19)	humble prayer or entreaty	Looking for a sign from God, Janie puts up her arms in an act of **supplication**.
archly (ch. 19)	in a cunning, crafty, or mischievous way	Janie responds to Tea Cake's compliments **archly**.
pallet (ch. 19)	a mattress of straw or other small, makeshift bed	Because the doctor advises her not to share the bed with Tea Cake, Janie sleeps on a **pallet** instead.
bailiff (ch. 19)	an officer in a court of law who helps the judge control the courtroom	Janie's former friends tell the **bailiff** that they want to testify against her.
fetid (ch. 20)	having an unpleasant odor	Janie airs out the **fetid** house so that it no longer seems full of bad feelings.

Name _____

Date _____

Understanding Vocabulary Words

Directions: The following words appear in this section of the book. Use context clues and reference materials to determine an accurate definition for each word.

Word	Definition
subtleties (ch. 18)	
grotesques (ch. 18)	
oblique (ch. 18)	
hackles (ch. 18)	
disgorged (ch. 19)	
supplication (ch. 19)	
archly (ch. 19)	
pallet (ch. 19)	
bailiff (ch. 19)	
fetid (ch. 20)	

Name _____

Date _____

During-Reading Vocabulary Activity

Directions: As you read these chapters, choose five important words from the story. Then, use those five words to complete this word flow chart. On each arrow, write a vocabulary word. In the boxes between the words, explain how the words connect. An example for the words *grotesques* and *subtleties* has been done for you.

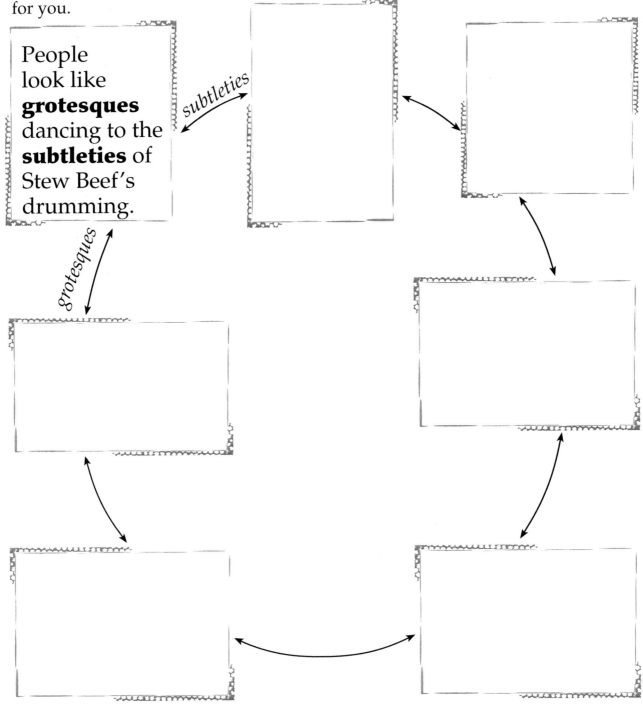

People look like **grotesques** dancing to the **subtleties** of Stew Beef's drumming.

Analyzing the Literature

Provided below are discussion questions you can use in small groups, with the whole class, or for written assignments. Each question is given at two levels so you can choose the right question for each group of students. Activity sheets with these questions are provided (pages 58–59) if you want students to write their responses. For each question, a few key discussion points are provided for your reference.

Story Element	■ Level 1	▲ Level 2	Key Discussion Points
Setting	Would you have stayed on or left the muck after hearing the hurricane warnings if you were in Tea Cake and Janie's shoes? Explain your answer.	Do you sympathize with Tea Cake and Janie's decision to stay on the muck despite the hurricane warnings? Why or why not?	Students may say they would have heeded the warnings. Other students may argue that it is normal for people to underestimate storms and think "it won't happen to me." Some may sympathize with Tea Cake's desire not to break up the party or give up the income he was receiving from the bean crops.
Plot	How and why are the bodies of the black and white hurricane victims treated differently? What do you think should be done instead?	"Death is the great equalizer." Argue that this statement is true or false based on events that happen in these chapters of the novel.	When Tea Cake is forced to bury the dead, he is made to handle the bodies differently, according to race. Only white bodies are given coffins, as there are not enough coffins for all. Many of the bodies are so damaged that it is almost impossible to tell the victim's racial background.
Character	How does Janie's newfound ability to speak up for herself and tell her own story prove important in the last chapters of the novel?	Janie learns to speak up and tell her own story. Argue that this is or is not the most important thing she learns in the novel.	Janie tells her story in the courtroom, thus saving herself. At the end of the novel, we see her telling the story of her adventures to Pheoby, who feels that she has learned an immense amount from listening to Janie.
Character	Do you think that Janie will be happy now that she has returned to her house in Eatonville? Why or why not?	Predict what Janie's future will hold. Will she be content in her house and in Eatonville? How might her life be different from before?	In the closing paragraphs of the novel, Janie seems content to be home. The memories of Tea Cake make her house a place she likes to be. Students may predict that Janie's role in the town will now be different, as she has learned to speak up for herself and care less about what others think.

Name _____

Date _____

Analyzing the Literature

Directions: Think about the section you just read. Read each question and state your response with textual evidence.

1. Would you have stayed on or left the muck after hearing the hurricane warnings if you were in Tea Cake and Janie's shoes? Explain your answer.

_____

_____

_____

_____

2. How and why are the bodies of the black and white hurricane victims treated differently? What do you think should be done instead?

_____

_____

_____

_____

3. How does Janie's newfound ability to speak up for herself and tell her own story prove important in the last chapters of the novel?

_____

_____

_____

4. Do you think that Janie will be happy now that she has returned to her house in Eatonville? Why or why not?

_____

_____

_____

Name _____

Date _____

▲ Analyzing the Literature

Directions: Think about the section you just read. Read each question and state your response with textual evidence.

1. Do you sympathize with Tea Cake and Janie's decision to stay on the muck despite the hurricane warnings? Why or why not?

_____

_____

_____

_____

2. "Death is the great equalizer." Argue that this statement is true or false based on events that happen in these chapters of the novel.

_____

_____

_____

_____

3. Janie learns to speak up and tell her own story. Argue that this is or is not the most important thing she learns in the novel.

_____

_____

_____

_____

4. Predict what Janie's future will hold. Will she be content in her house and in Eatonville? How might her life be different from before?

_____

_____

_____

Name _____

Date _____

Reader Response

Directions: Choose one of the following prompts about this section to answer. Be sure you include a topic sentence in your response, use textual evidence to support your opinion, and provide a strong conclusion that summarizes your opinion.

Writing Prompts

- **Narrative Piece**—Describe your most memorable and/or dramatic experience of being in a storm. Compare and contrast your experience with that of Janie and Tea Cake.
- **Argument Piece**—Argue that *Their Eyes Were Watching God* is or is not a tragic novel. Use textual evidence throughout your argument.

_____

_____

_____

_____

_____

_____

_____

_____

_____

_____

_____

_____

_____

_____

Name _____

Date _____

Close Reading the Literature

Directions: Closely reread the passage from chapter 18 starting with the paragraph that begins, "Sometime that night the winds came back . . . ." Stop with the paragraph that ends, "He turned back to tell Janie about it so she could be ready to go." Read each question and then revisit the text to find evidence that supports your answer.

1. What examples of personification do you see in this passage?

_____

_____

_____

2. Why do the people feel safe despite what is going on with the weather? Cite the text in your answer.

_____

_____

_____

3. Point to specific details in the text that show us or tell us how the world is suddenly changed by the hurricane.

_____

_____

_____

4. Is Janie angry with Tea Cake for having exposed her to this disastrous situation? Why or why not? Support your answer with textual evidence.

_____

_____

_____

Name _____

Date _____

Making Connections–The Hero's Journey

Directions: "The Hero's Journey" is a narrative pattern identified in 1949 by American scholar Joseph Campbell that can frequently be found in myths, fairy tales, and religious stories, as well as in contemporary novels and movies. Look at the stages below and think about Janie's adventures in *Their Eyes Were Watching God*. On another sheet of paper, answer these questions: Does Janie go on a hero's journey? Which, if any, of her experiences correspond with the stages below?

1. **The hero is in the ordinary world.** He or she may be dissatisfied and long for adventure.

2. **A herald brings a call to adventure.** The hero may resist the call at first.

3. **The hero makes a conscious decision to embark on an adventure.**

4. **The hero enters a strange, dream-like realm.** Everything is topsy-turvy here. It is very different from the ordinary world to which the hero is accustomed.

5. **The hero makes his or her way down a "road of trials."** He or she may encounter helpers.

6. **The hero makes a "night sea voyage," a significant voyage, often across water and/or at night.**

7. **The hero has a showdown with something big and bad and through this confrontation learns to view himself/herself in a new way.** He/she may have to die (literally or symbolically) and be reborn.

8. **The hero returns to the ordinary world with some important magical item or a newfound piece of knowledge (called "the boon").** The hero may encounter fresh obstacles during this return.

9. **Back in the ordinary world, the hero shares "the boon" with others.**

Name

Date

Creating with the Story Elements

Directions: Thinking about the story elements of character, setting, and plot in a novel is very important to understanding what is happening and why. Complete **one** of the following activities based on what you've read so far. Be creative and have fun!

Characters

Make a collage, drawing, or painting that commemorates Tea Cake's personality and life. Be ready to explain the various elements that you have included in your piece of artwork.

Setting

Write about the hurricane from the perspective of the personified Lake Okeechobee. Write in prose or compose a poetic dramatic monologue in which the lake is the poem's speaker.

Plot

Write an account of Janie's trial as it would appear in a newspaper. If you wish, print out your typed story in a newspaper-style format. Include a headline, columns of text, and a photograph or an artist's sketch.

Name _____

Date _____

Post-Reading Theme Thoughts

Directions: Read each of the statements in the first column. Choose a main character from *Their Eyes Were Watching God*. Think about that character's point of view. From that character's perspective, decide if the character would agree or disagree with the statements. Record the character's opinion by marking an X in Agree or Disagree for each statement. Explain your choices in the fourth column using text evidence.

Character I Chose: _____

Statement	Agree	Disagree	Explain Your Answer
Physical comforts and financial security are not what make a person happy.			
A person who really loves you will want you to learn new things and express yourself.			
You can't live life by standing still. You have to set out on the road and take a risk.			
Envy is dangerous because it makes people believe the worst when they should know better.			

Name _____

Date _____

Culminating Activity 1:
Imaginary Talk Show

Directions: Imagine that Zora Neale Hurston and characters from *Their Eyes Were Watching God* are about to appear on a television talk show. What questions would you like the host to ask them? Brainstorm a list of questions on the lines below.

_____

_____

_____

_____

_____

_____

_____

_____

_____

_____

Together with classmates, organize and present an imaginary talk show in which author Zora Neale Hurston and characters from *Their Eyes Were Watching God* appear as guests. Decide on the set and staging elements for your talk show. Decide who will play the part of the talk show host, Hurston, and the characters from the novel. Create a script or a basic outline of events for the show. Select audience questions to be asked during the show, and create answers for them.

Name _____

Date _____

Culminating Activity 2: *Their Eyes Were Watching God* in a Nutshell

Directions: Describe the plot of *Their Eyes Were Watching God* in as few sentences as possible, but without leaving out major events or crucial information about the characters. Make a draft of your summary on the lines below. Then, edit what you've written. Can you make your summary brief and precise enough so that it fits on an index card? On a business card? See how succinct you can be.

_____

_____

_____

_____

_____

_____

_____

_____

_____

_____

_____

_____

_____

_____

_____

_____

Name _____

Date _____

Comprehension Assessment

Directions: Circle the letter for the best response to each question.

1. Which of the following sentences summarizes a main theme of *Their Eyes Were Watching God*?

    A. It's easier to love a rich man than a poor one.

    B. Parents and grandparents know what is best for children.

    C. Life is a journey to the horizons in search of the people who help you grow.

    D. It's always better to play it safe than take a chance that might end in disaster.

2. Which quotation from the book provides the best evidence of your answer for number 1?

    E. "Somebody got to think for women and chillun and chickens and cows."

    F. "It's a known fact, Pheoby, you got tuh go there tuh know there."

    G. "A pretty doll baby like you is made to sit on de front porch and rock and fan yo'self."

    H. "Dat's de very prong all us black women gits hung on. Dis love! Dat's just whut's got us uh pullin' and uh haulin' and uh sweatin' . . . ."

3. What is the main idea of the passage below?

    > She went over to the dresser and looked hard at her skin and features. The young girl was gone, but a handsome woman had taken her place. She tore off the kerchief from her head and let down her plentiful hair.

    A. Janie is uncomfortable in her own skin.

    B. Janie feels freer to be herself now that Joe has died.

    C. Janie feels unable to be herself now that Joe has died.

    D. Janie wishes she were a young girl again.

4. Choose **two** details from those below to support your answer to number 3.

    E. The head rag has always irritated Janie.

    F. Matt Bonner's mule dies after it is freed.

    G. The Indians are leaving because of the hurricane.

    H. Joe insisted that Janie remain quiet and cover her hair.

Comprehension Assessment (cont.)

5. Which statement best expresses the reason why Janie shoots Tea Cake?

   A. She is jealous that he has had an affair with another woman.

   B. She is tricked by the townspeople into shooting Tea Cake.

   C. She accidentally shoots Tea Cake while they are hunting.

   D. She shoots Tea Cake in self-defense.

6. What is the significance of the episode from *Their Eyes Were Watching God* described below?

   > The dog stood up and growled like a lion, stiff-standing hackles, stiff muscles, teeth uncovered as he lashed up his fury for the charge. Tea Cake split the water like an otter, opening his knife as he dived.

   _____

   _____

   _____

7. Which statement best expresses a reoccurring theme from *Their Eyes Were Watching God*?

   E. Women and children should be seen and not heard.

   F. People with little money have little fun.

   G. Marriage shouldn't be about physical comforts and financial security.

   H. Weather reports are sometimes wrong.

8. What quotation below provides support for your answer to number 7?

   A. Janie: "Ah done lived Grandma's way, and now Ah means tuh live mine."

   B. Tea Cake: "Ah wants tuh see if Ah kin hear anything 'bout de boys from de Glades. Maybe dey all come through all right. Maybe not."

   C. Jody: "Ah'm buyin' in here, and buyin' in big. Soon's we find some place to sleep tonight us menfolks got to call people together and form a committee."

   D. Nanny: "Ah raked and scraped and bought dis lil piece uh land so you wouldn't have to stay in de white folks' yard and tuck yo' head befo' other chillun at school."

Name _____

Date _____

Response to Literature:
Considering the Author's Purpose

Now that you have completed reading *Their Eyes Were Watching God*, think about why Hurston may have chosen to write this particular novel. What was she trying to say or do? What was her purpose?

Directions: On the lines below, describe what you think Hurston's main purpose was in writing *Their Eyes Were Watching God*. Support your argument with ample evidence from the text. If you believe that Hurston had more than one purpose in mind, describe her different possible motives for writing the book. Then, using textual evidence, argue which purpose you believe was most important to Hurston.

_____
_____
_____
_____
_____
_____
_____
_____
_____
_____
_____
_____
_____

Name _____

Date _____

Response to Literature Rubric

Directions: Use this rubric to evaluate student responses.

	Exceptional Writing	Quality Writing	Developing Writing
Focus and Organization	☐ States a clear opinion and elaborates well. Engages the reader from the opening hook through the middle to the conclusion. Demonstrates clear understanding of the intended audience and purpose of the piece.	☐ Provides a clear and consistent opinion. Maintains a clear perspective and supports it through elaborating details. Makes the opinion clear in the opening hook and summarizes well in the conclusion.	☐ Provides an inconsistent point of view. Does not support the topic adequately or misses pertinent information. Provides lack of clarity in the beginning, middle, and conclusion.
Text Evidence	☐ Provides comprehensive and accurate support. Includes relevant and worthwhile text references.	☐ Provides limited support. Provides few supporting text references.	☐ Provides very limited support for the text. Provides no supporting text references.
Written Expression	☐ Uses descriptive and precise language with clarity and intention. Maintains a consistent voice and uses an appropriate tone that supports meaning. Uses multiple sentence types and transitions well between ideas.	☐ Uses a broad vocabulary. Maintains a consistent voice and supports a tone and feelings through language. Varies sentence length and word choices.	☐ Uses a limited and unvaried vocabulary. Provides an inconsistent or weak voice and tone. Provides little to no variation in sentence type and length.
Language Conventions	☐ Capitalizes, punctuates, and spells accurately. Demonstrates complete thoughts within sentences, with accurate subject-verb agreement. Uses paragraphs appropriately and with clear purpose.	☐ Capitalizes, punctuates, and spells accurately. Demonstrates complete thoughts within sentences and appropriate grammar. Paragraphs are properly divided and supported.	☐ Incorrectly capitalizes, punctuates, and spells. Uses fragmented or run-on sentences. Utilizes poor grammar overall. Paragraphs are poorly divided and developed.

The responses provided here are just examples of what the students may answer. Many accurate responses are possible for the questions throughout this unit.

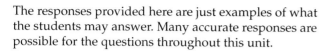

During-Reading Vocabulary Activity—Section 1:
Chapters 1–4 (page 16)

1. Johnny Taylor is described as **shiftless**, meaning that he is lazy and lacks ambition.

2. Janie's **conjectures** are that her feelings about Logan will change and she will learn to love him.

Close Reading the Literature—Section 1:
Chapters 1–4 (page 21)

1. Joe is described as a "cityfied, stylish dressed man with his hat set at an angle that didn't belong in [those] parts." We are told that he carries a coat over his arm and wears a shirt with "silk sleeveholders." He is "seal-brown," but Janie thinks he acts like Mr. Washburn or "somebody like that." The details tell us that Joe has some money and that he wants to look like he has money. He exudes an air of control and confidence.

2. Joe says he is going to a town in Florida that is made "all outa colored folks." He wants to move there and "buy in big." By making investments with saved money, he plans to become a "big voice" in the new town.

3. Joe does not "represent sun-up and pollen and blooming trees," instead he "[speaks] for far horizon" and for "change and chance."

4. It is questionable whether Janie is in love with Joe or feels great desire for him. This is suggested by the comment that he does not "represent…pollen and blooming trees." Joe represents a chance for her to leave and see more of the world and experience an adventure.

Making Connections—Section 1:
Chapters 1–4 (page 22)

Students' responses will vary, but should be similar to:

1. I bet they are talking about me right now.

2. She looked like she had been suffering for a long time without anything good happening.

3. Why do you look so unhappy?

4. If you think I want to take you away so that I can abuse and mistreat you, you're wrong.

During-Reading Vocabulary Activity—Section 2:
Chapters 5–7 (page 26)

1. Janie has been quiet most of the time, so the people are surprised when she makes a moving speech in chapter 6.

2. A person with **stolidness** will not react strongly to either an insult or a compliment. Like the earth, he or she will "soak up" whatever is said with "the same indifference."

Close Reading the Literature—Section 2:
Chapters 5–7 (page 31)

1. In the first paragraph, Janie is described as "a rut in the road." The implication is that she is stuck and not moving, and that she has been worn down and pounded into the ground. In the second paragraph, Janie thinks of "a country road at sun-up and consider[s] flight." The road here seems to be a metaphor for escape and change.

2. Janie doesn't realize that she is "the world and the heavens boiled down to a drop. Man attempting to climb to painless heights from the dung hill." She might realize through reading about fictional characters or figures from history how much she is like all other people in her desire to better herself and her life.

3. One of the parts is "going about tending store and prostrating itself before Jody," while the other part sits "under a shady tree with the wind blowing through her hair and her clothes." She splits herself to make life bearable, so that she can accept what is happening.

4. He talks about her age because "he doesn't want her to stay young while he [grows] old." He is worried about the fact that he is aging badly and was already older than her to begin with. He is insecure and is "hurting inside."

Close Reading the Literature—Section 3:
Chapters 8–12 (page 41)

1. On the outside, Janie is keeping a formal and appropriate appearance, her face "starched and ironed." Her expensive veil is like a wall she hides behind. Inside she is experiencing "resurrection and new life" and "springtime."

2. The house "creaks and cries all night under the weight of lonesomeness." It is a double for Janie, who is also feeling alone and emotional.

3. Janie doesn't go back because she "has no interest" in her "seldom-seen mother" and hates her grandmother for having pushed her into the miserable early marriage. She feels she has no reason to return.

4. Janie thinks she should have been making a journey to find people. Instead, she has "run off down a back road after things." She blames Nanny, seeing her as a kind of person who "loves to deal in scraps."

Making Connections—Section 3:
Chapters 8–12 (page 42)

Students may list the following examples:

- Death: described as having toes, standing in a house, watching the world;

- Rumor: described as a "wingless bird"

- The walls: described as squeezing Janie's breath out

During-Reading Vocabulary Activity—Section 4:
Chapters 13–17 (page 46)

1. A person would drink, dance, and listen to music at a **jook**.

2. A **transient** person travels from place to place and has no consistent home.

Close Reading the Literature—Section 4:
Chapters 13–17 (page 51)

1. Tea Cake teaches Janie to shoot. He sees no reason for her not to learn. He wants her to be able to hunt for game and also comments that there is "always some trashy rascal dat needs uh good killin'."

2. People are attracted to the house because Tea Cake sits in the doorway playing guitar. Also, Tea Cake is "always laughing and full of fun."

3. She goes to the fields because Tea Cake claims he is lonesome without her. Janie claims she likes being out in the fields, saying, "it's mo' nicer than settin' round dese quarters all day."

4. It has been assumed that she considers herself "too good to work like the rest of the women." The others change their minds when they see Janie "romping and playing" behind the boss's back.

Close Reading the Literature—Section 5:
Chapters 18–20 (page 61)

1. "The mists" are personified when they "arm themselves . . . to march forth." The lake is personified when it is described as a "monster" rolling "in his bed." Night is described as "striding . . . with the whole world in his hands." The thunder and lightning are personified when described as "Massa draw[ing] him chair upstairs."

2. The African American workers feel safe because the "people in the big houses" haven't evacuated. If the wealthier people feel secure, the workers think they have no reason to worry.

3. The baby rabbit enters their house for shelter. The wind and water seem to have given "life to lots of things that folks think of as dead and given death to so much that had been living things." There are "stray fish swimming in the yard."

4. Janie is not angry. She believes that a person cannot die "till dey time come nohow." She says that whatever happens, she is thankful for her two years with Tea Cake. She feels better off than the "so many people" who "never [see] the light at all."

Making Connections—Section 5:
Chapters 18–20 (page 62)

Some students may say that Janie resists the first call to adventure when she enters into the marriage to Logan Killicks. She makes a conscious decision to embark on adventure when she sets off with Tea Cake. Students may see a "night sea voyage" in the flood scene. The scene in which Tea Cake is shot may be interpreted as the big "showdown." Students may note how Pheoby feels educated and enlightened after listening to Janie. This can be interpreted as Janie "sharing the boon."

Comprehension Assessment (pages 67–68)

1. C. Life is a journey to the horizons in search of the people who help you grow.

2. F. "It's a known fact, Pheoby, you got tuh go there tuh know there."

3. B. Janie feels freer to be herself now that Joe has died.

4. E. The head rag has always irritated Janie. H. Joe insisted that Janie remain quiet and cover her hair.

5. D. She shoots Tea Cake in self-defense.

6. The episode is significant because Tea Cake tries to save Janie from the dog but ends up getting bitten and contracting distemper. Janie later will have to shoot him to defend her own life. Some students may say it is the climax or a major turning point in the novel.

7. G. Marriage shouldn't be about physical comforts and financial security.

8. A. Janie: "Ah done lived Grandma's way, and now Ah means tuh live mine."